What I Like About TOADS

By JUDY HAWES

Illustrated by James and Ruth McCrea

Thomas Y. Crowell Company • New York

LET'S–READ–AND–FIND–OUT BOOK CLUB EDITION.

I didn't used to like toads.

I thought toads would give me warts.

Now I know better. I know how lucky I am
to have a toad in my garden.

I've learned a lot about toads.

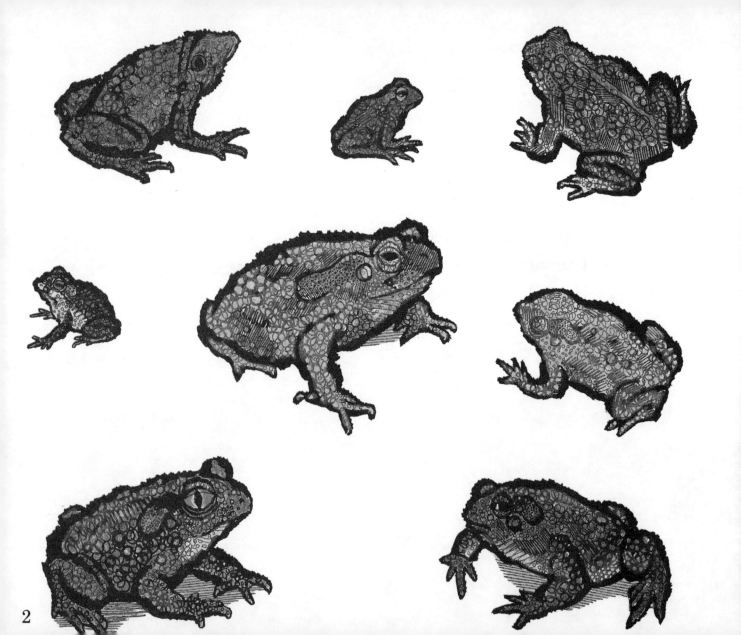

2

There are more than one hundred different kinds of toads.

This is my toad:

All toads are amphibians. That means they can live in water and on land.

Toads have tremendous appetites. They eat at night mostly. They stuff themselves with bugs and worms. During one summer, a single toad may eat 10,000 insects and 2,000 cutworms. One toad ate 86 houseflies in ten minutes!

Toads eat bugs and beetles, flies and mosquitoes. They eat all kinds of insects.

Every year toads save millions of dollars for farmers. In some countries farmers buy toads to eat the bugs that eat their crops.

9

A toad's skin is dry and covered with warts.

I still don't like the warts on toads but I know that
toads can't give me warts.
Just the same, I handle toads gently because they
can give off poison.

If a toad is frightened a white liquid oozes through its skin. This liquid comes from two glands behind the toad's eyes. This liquid will not give you warts, but it may sting.

The toad uses this poison to protect himself. If a dog catches a toad in his teeth, he drops it *fast*. The toad's poison burns the dog's mouth. Dogs soon learn to leave toads alone.

I have read about a giant toad that gives off a poison so strong it can kill a dog or blind a man. This is the "mariner" toad. It is twice as big as my toad. I don't think I could learn to like a giant toad.

Toads have other tricks to protect themselves. They
can puff themselves up and stretch out their hind
legs. This makes toads look too big for hungry
birds or snakes to eat.

The toad's color and shape protect him. Toads are usually a dull brown or gray with dark spots and streaks. They look like lumps of dirt to their enemies.

Toads can play dead very well. They can sit absolutely still for hours. No wonder their enemies can't see them. You can put a toad in any position and he will stay that way.

Insects are fooled, too, and may make the mistake of coming too close! Once a toad spots a victim he takes careful aim. He flicks out his sticky tongue and catches the insect. His tongue flicks out and back so fast, you cannot see it move. A toad has no teeth. He swallows his victims whole.

Toads feed mostly at night. During the day they
usually stay buried under leaves or loose dirt. My
toad hides under a stone.

Cold weather makes toads sleepy. In winter, common
toads sleep about three feet underground.

Toads wake up in the spring when the days and nights are warm again. Right away, they hop to the nearest pond. The male toads puff out their throats and grunt to attract mates.

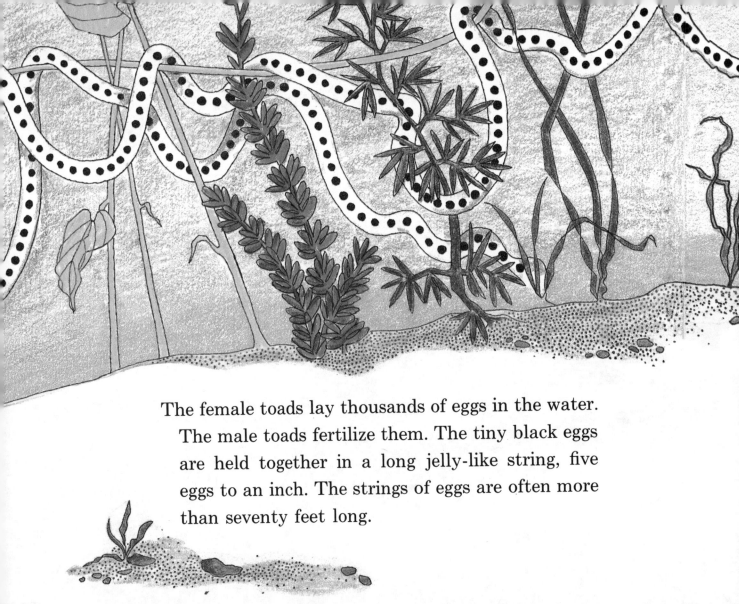

The female toads lay thousands of eggs in the water. The male toads fertilize them. The tiny black eggs are held together in a long jelly-like string, five eggs to an inch. The strings of eggs are often more than seventy feet long.

Within a few days, tiny black tadpoles hatch from the eggs. Soon the tadpoles grow back legs. Front legs appear next. The tadpoles' mouths grow bigger. Their long tails are slowly absorbed.

In six to nine weeks, the tadpoles have changed completely into little toadlets, less than half an inch long.

The new little toadlets hop ashore. There they hide for a week or two. At the first sudden shower, the toads appear like magic from behind every stone. It was once believed that they dropped like rain from the sky!

Now the young toads scatter. They leave the pond
to make their homes in woods or fields. There they
grow so quickly, they must shed their skins every
few weeks. By the time common toads are a year
old, they have grown to their full size of three
inches.

Few toads of any kind live to full adult size. These
lucky ones may live for twenty or thirty years!

What I like about toads is that they make good pets. They never wander far. They live in a small area. One man tells of a toad that lived in his garden for thirty-six years. It would come to him to have its back scratched.

Each night a toad returns to its favorite spot to feed. It might be near a lamppost or a lighted doorway where insects gather. My toad sits by the door of our screened porch.

I like toads better than frogs for pets. A frog can get
away from you in a flash. A frog can make big
jumps with his long back legs.

A toad has short back legs. He can't make big jumps.
He can only hop.

I like toads because of their pretty eyes. Toads' eyes are shiny black, marked with glistening gold. People used to think toads had real jewels in their heads.

I like toads because of their cheerful song. In springtime the air is filled with the toad's music.

There are a lot of things I like about toads. I hope you like them too.

ABOUT THE AUTHOR

Mrs. Hawes, mother of four, has worked with children as a teacher and as a leader in scouting and Sunday school. She now teaches a public school class for handicapped children. A native of Forest Hills, New York, she was graduated from Vassar College. Mrs. Hawes and her husband are residents of Glen Rock, New Jersey, where they participate in many community activities.

She is the author of six other titles in the Let's-Read-and-Find-Out science series: *Bees and Beelines; Fireflies in the Night; Watch Honeybees with Me; Shrimps; Ladybug, Ladybug, Fly Away Home;* and *Why Frogs Are Wet.*

ABOUT THE ILLUSTRATORS

Ruth McCrea was born in Jersey City, New Jersey. Her husband is a native of Peoria, Illinois. They both attended the Ringling School of Art in Sarasota, Florida, and took night classes at New York University and at The Brooklyn Museum. Mr. and Mrs. McCrea each grew up with an interest in writing and drawing. Since they met in art school, they have been working together on jacket design, writing, and illustrating. Mr. McCrea has also done book design and for several years taught typography at Cooper Union in New York City. Mrs. McCrea has illustrated many books on her own.

The McCreas, who have a son and two daughters, live in Bayport, New York.